001

002

Spiral designs

1

Floral motifs

Floral motifs

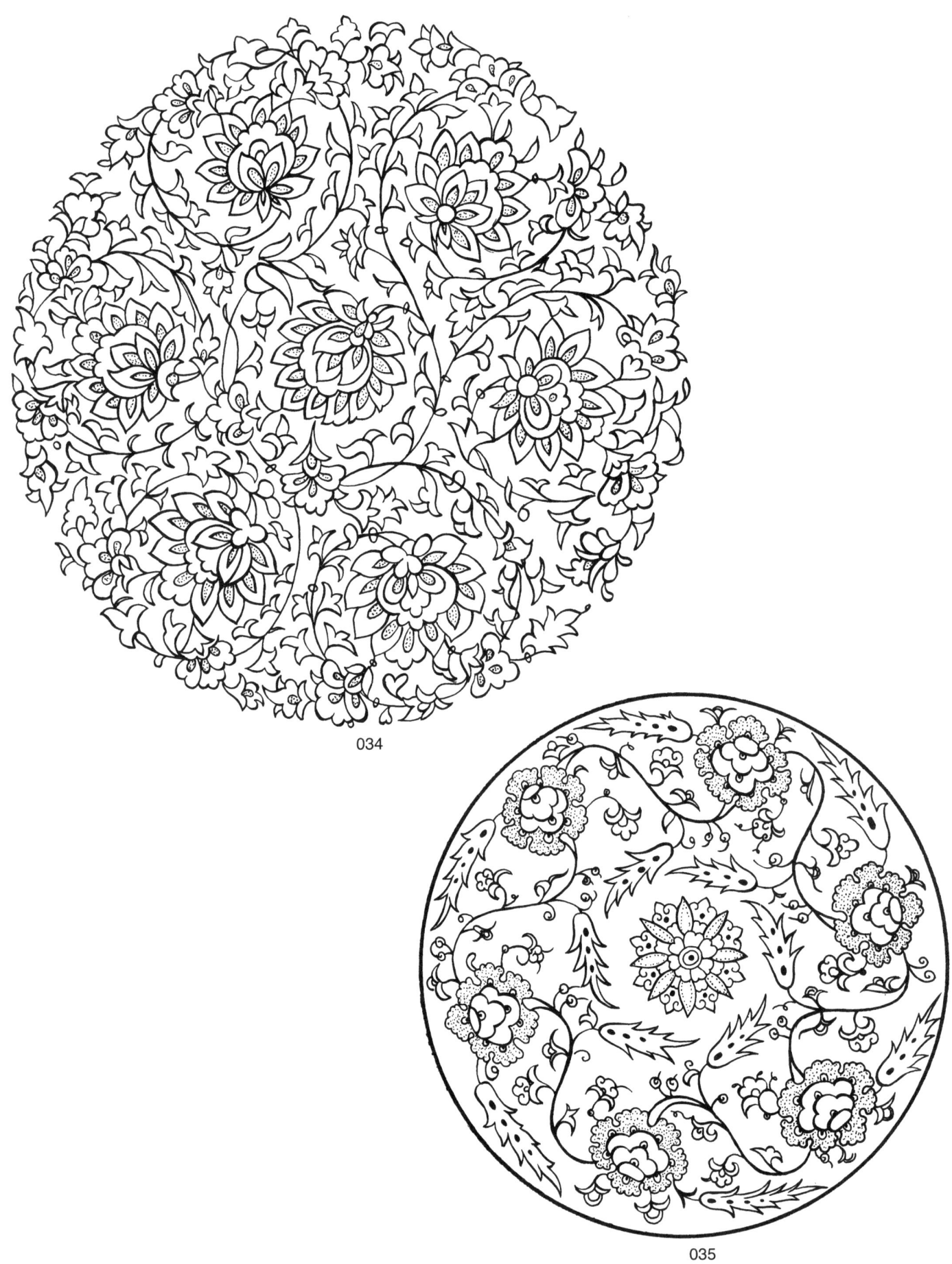

Floral motifs

Cloud scrolls

Cloud scrolls

Rounded floral motifs

Pointed floral motifs

Pomegranate motifs

Pomegranate motifs

Tulips

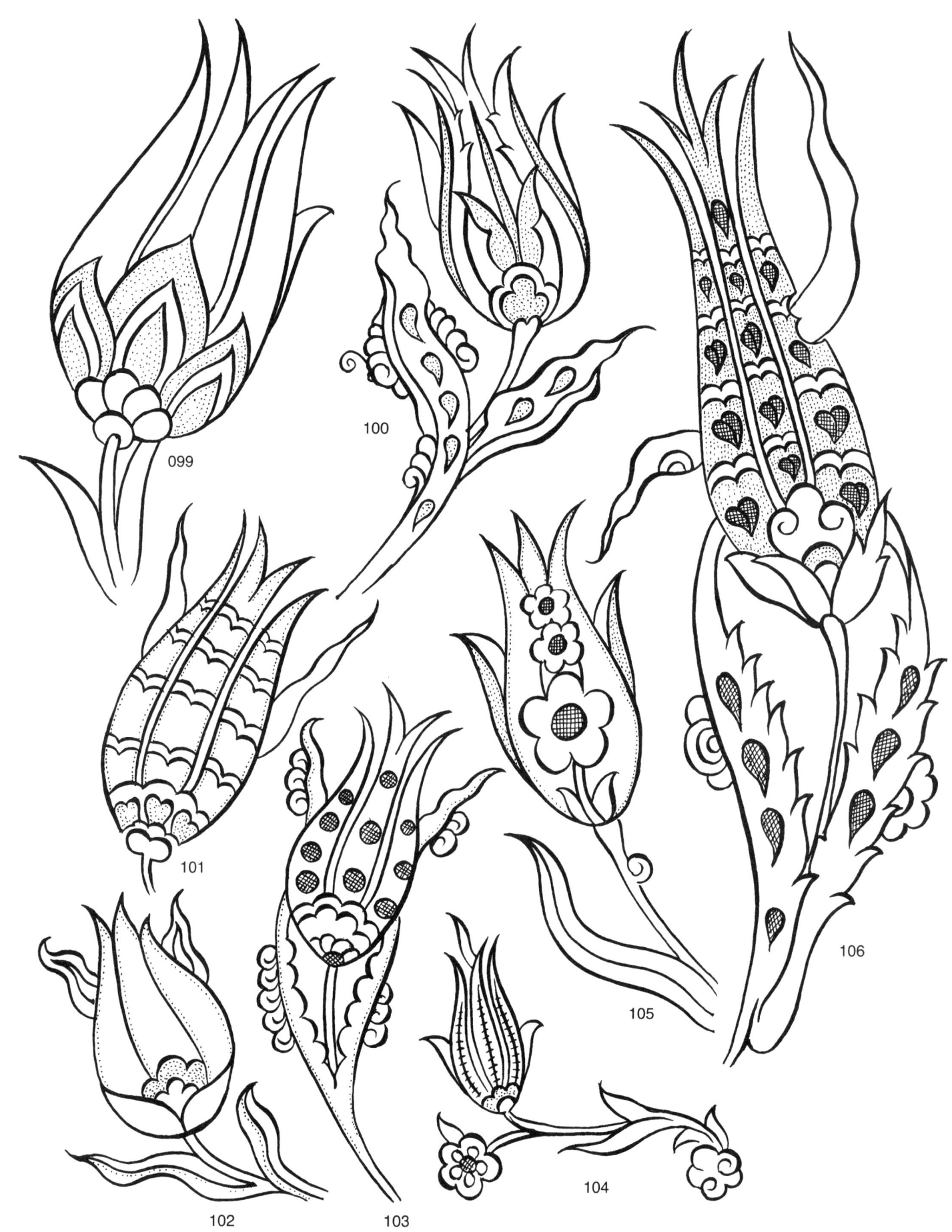

Tulips

Tulips

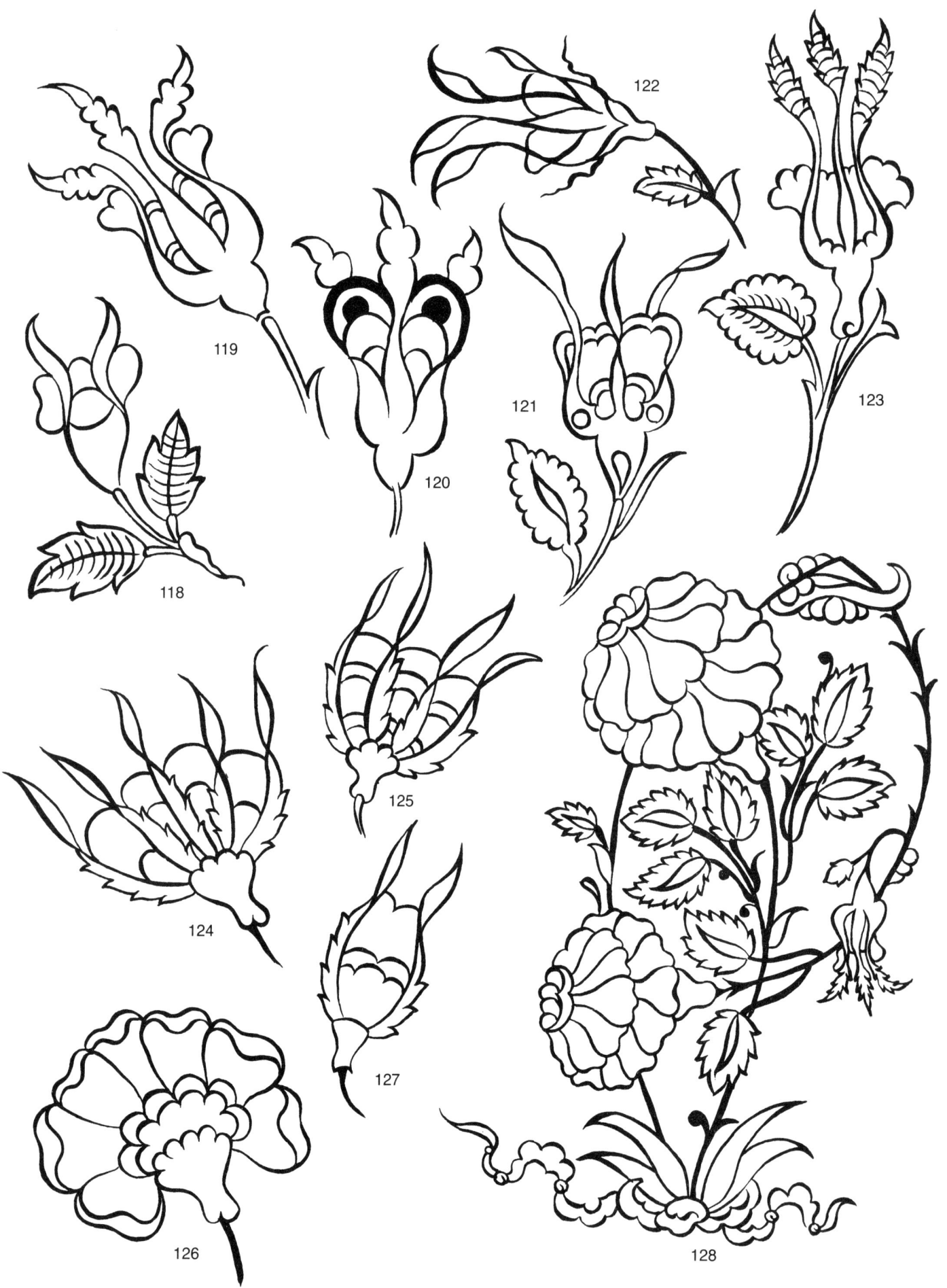

Rose and rosebud motifs

Rose and rosebud motifs

Carnation motifs

Carnation motifs

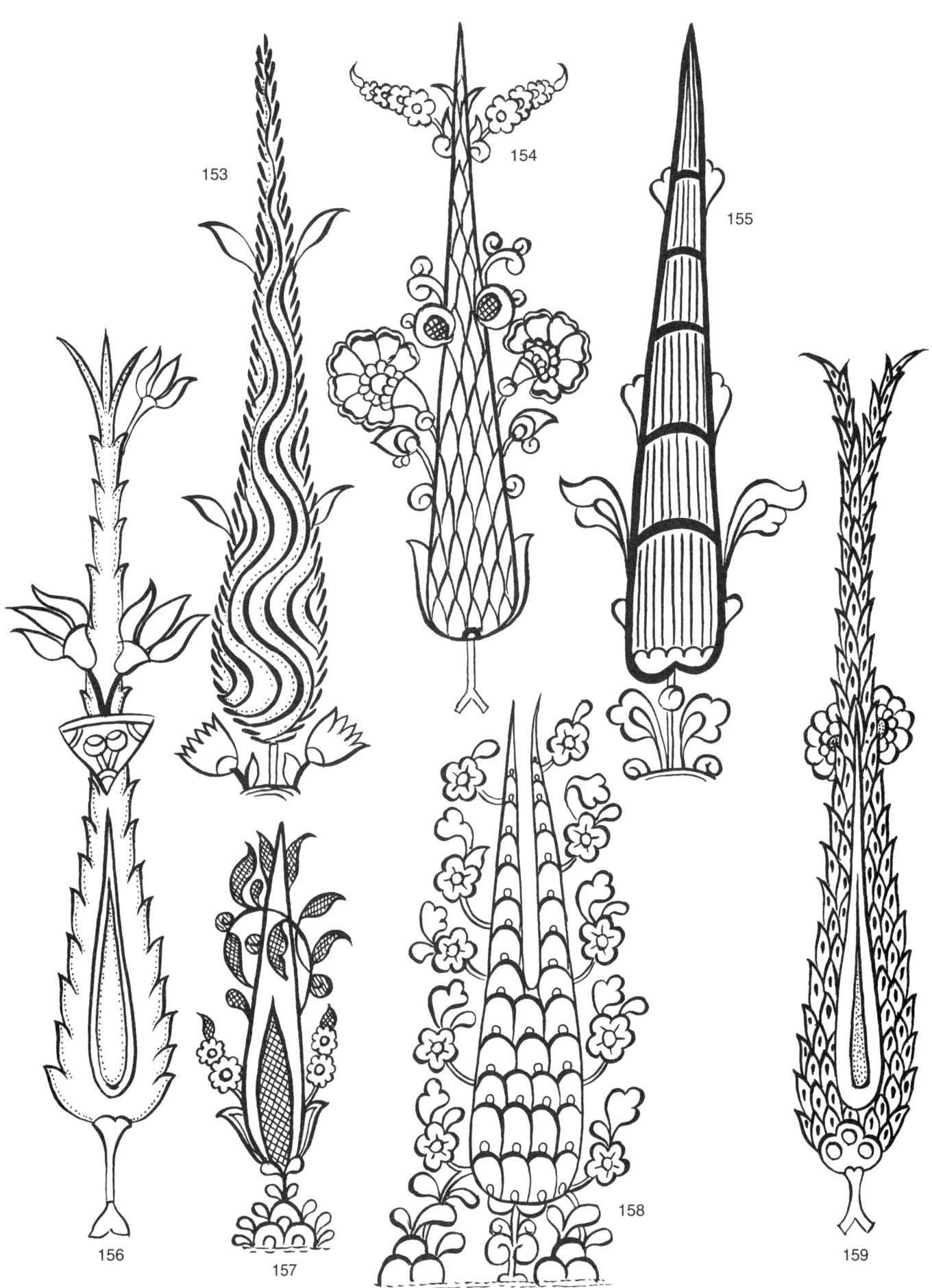

Cypress motifs

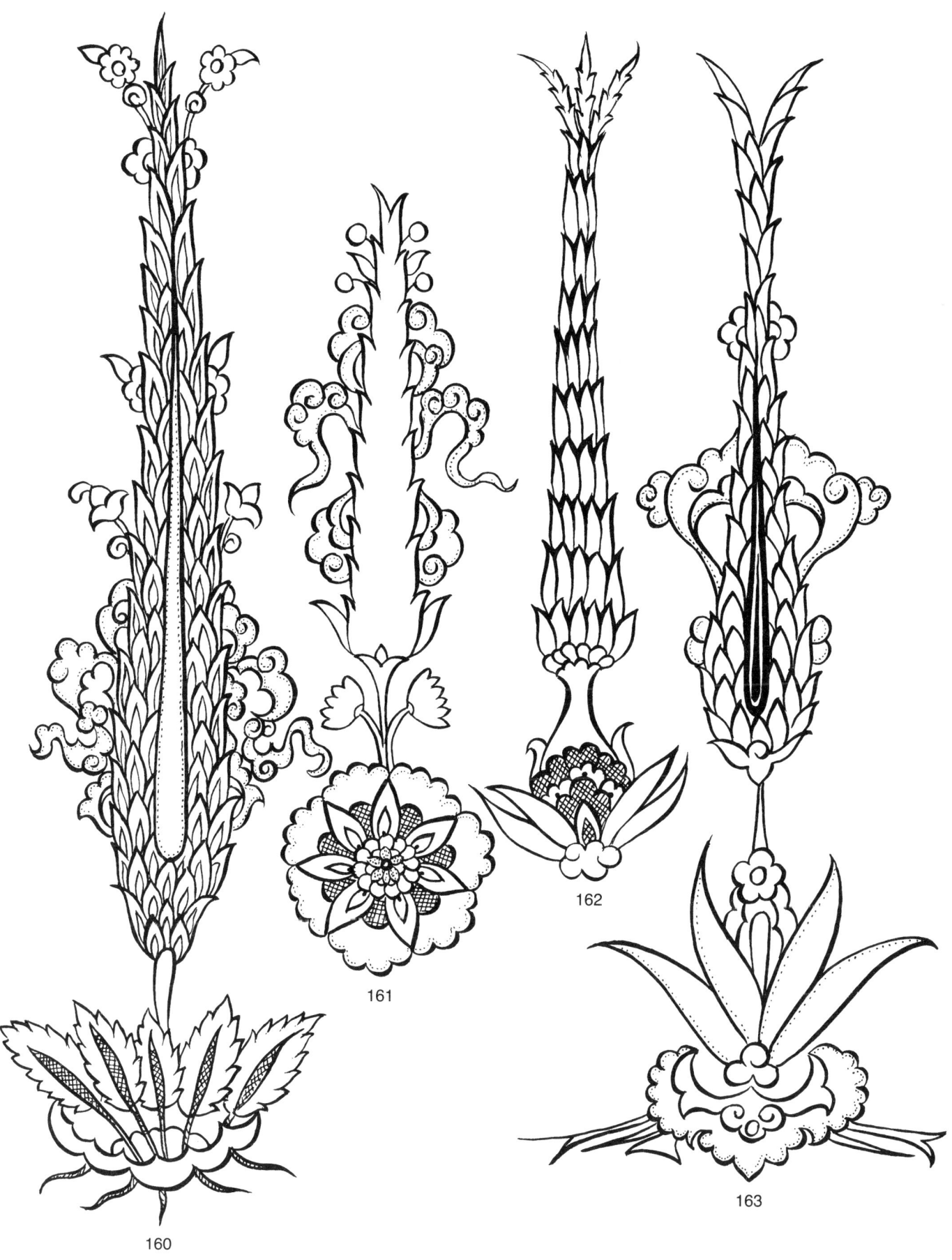

Cypress motifs

Clusters

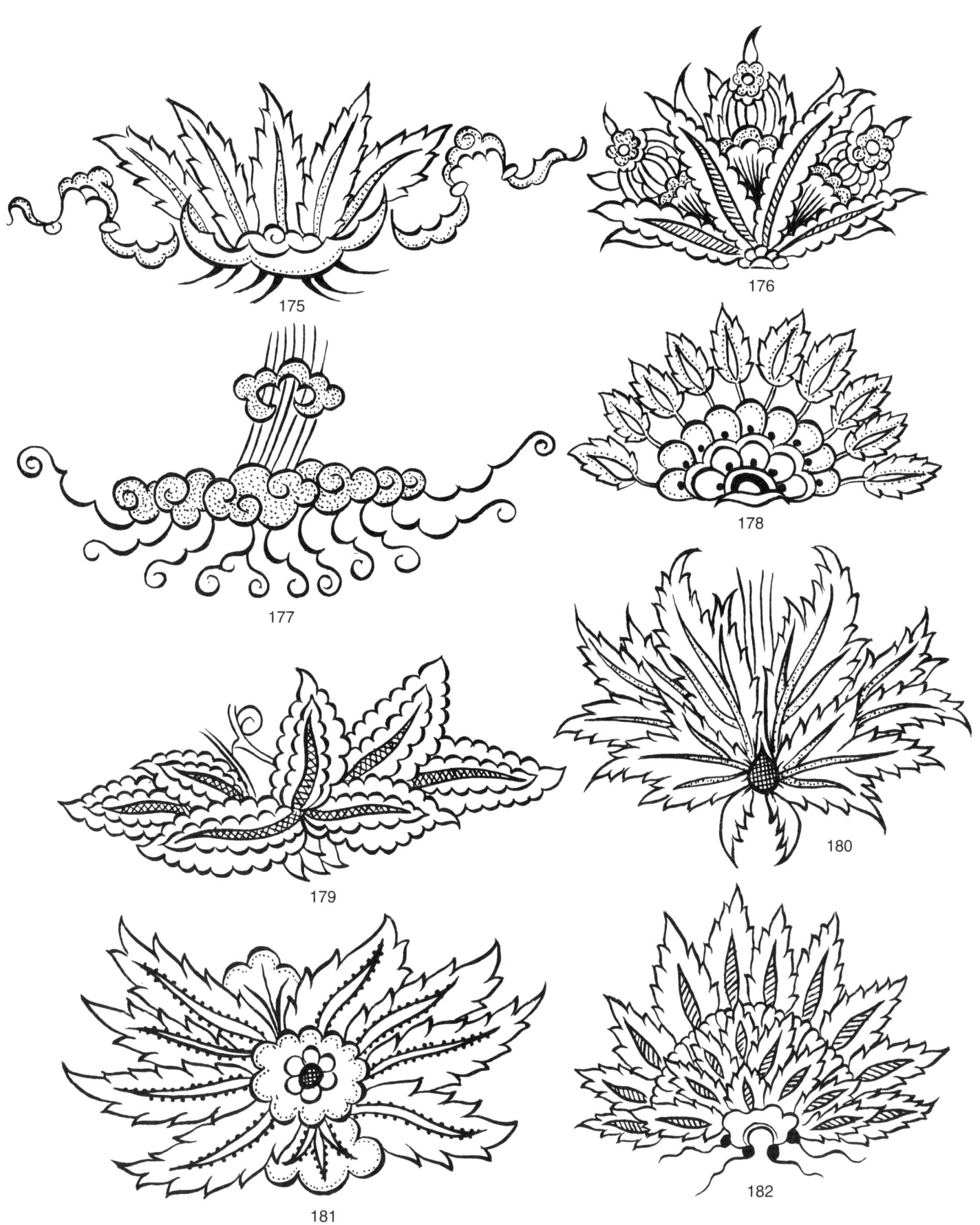

Clusters

Iris motifs

Various garden flowers

Hyacinths and similar flowers

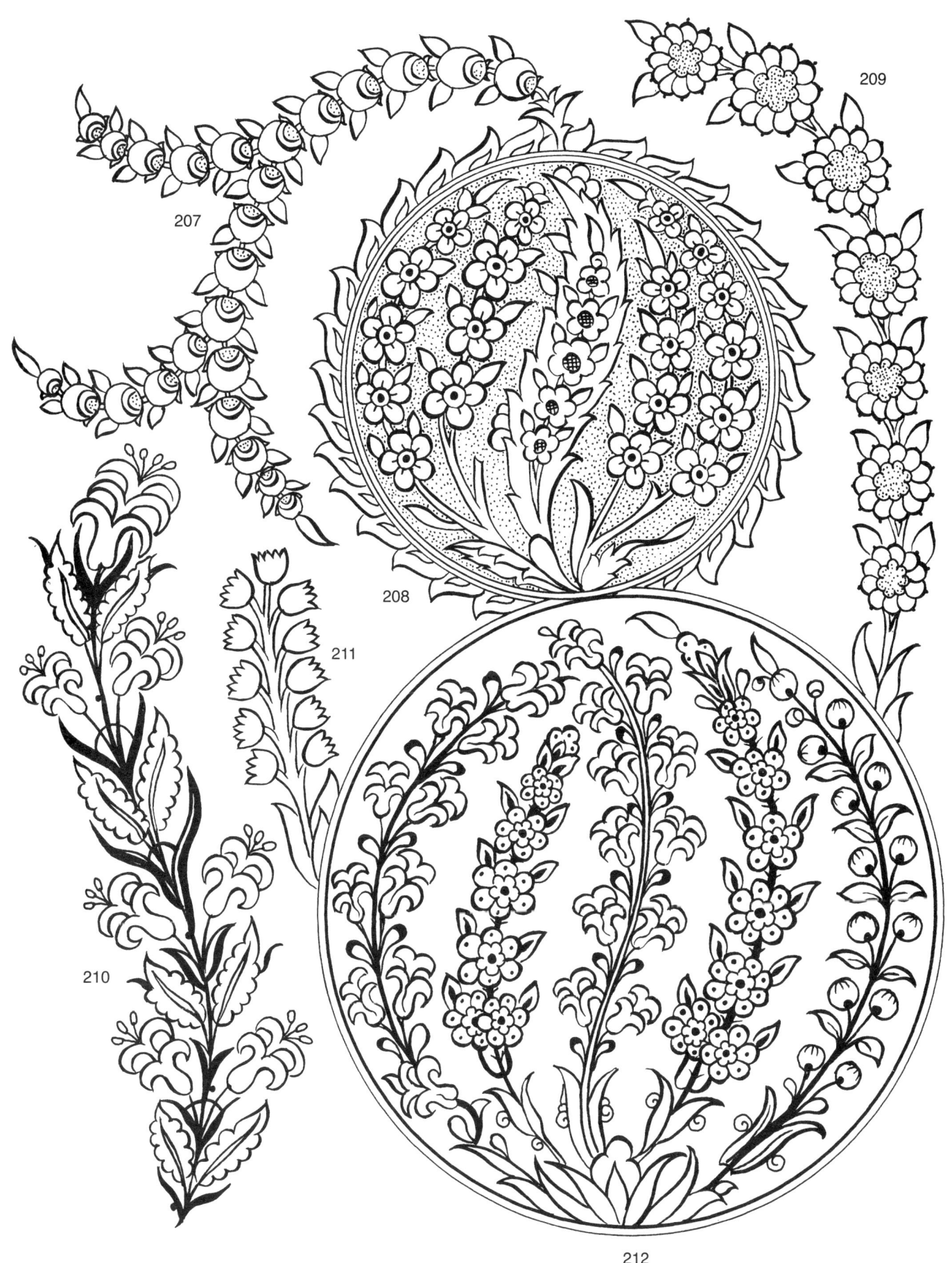

Hyacinths and similar flowers

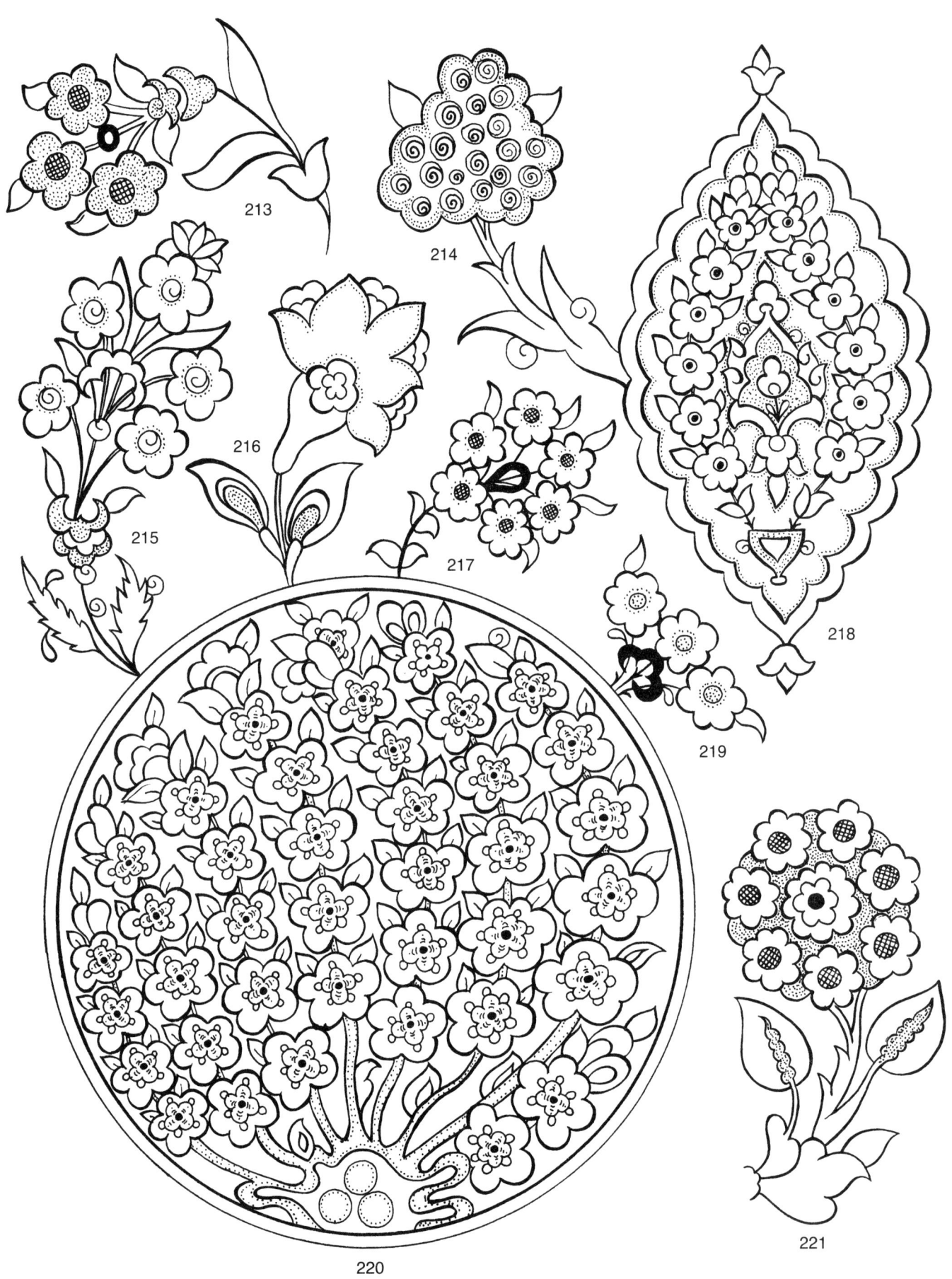

"Spring tree" and blossom motifs

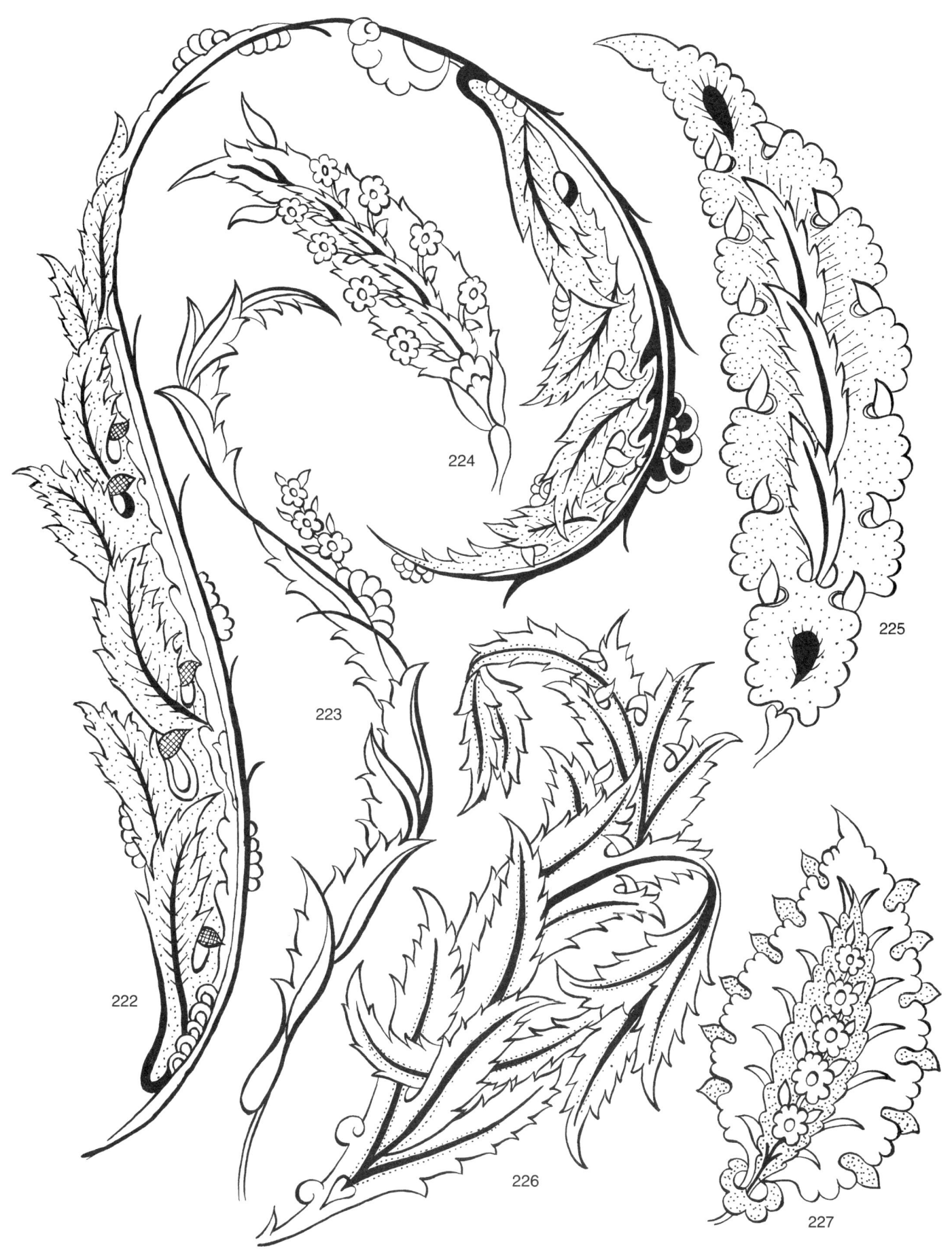

Saz (leaf) motifs

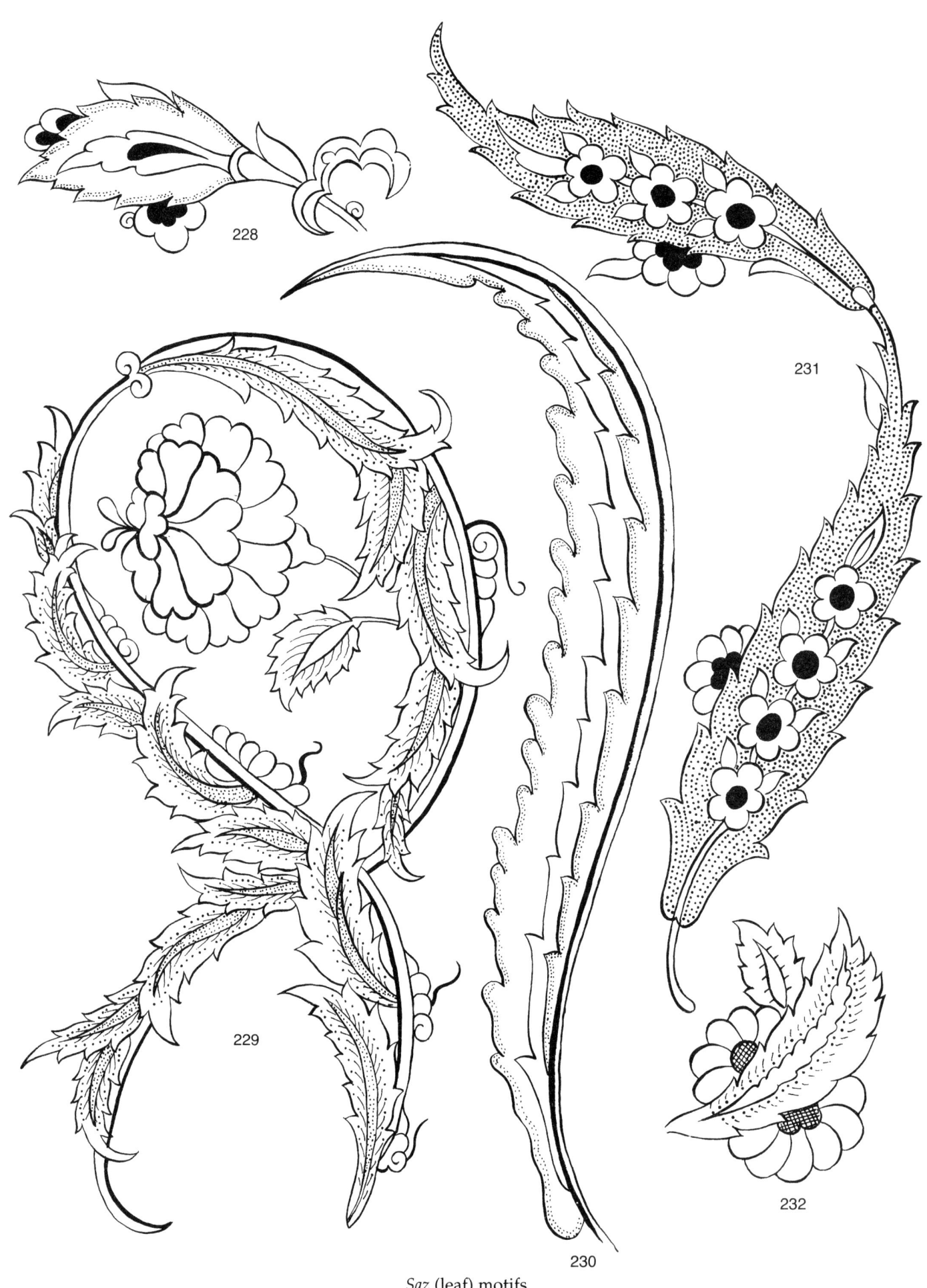

Saz (leaf) motifs

Saz (leaf) motifs

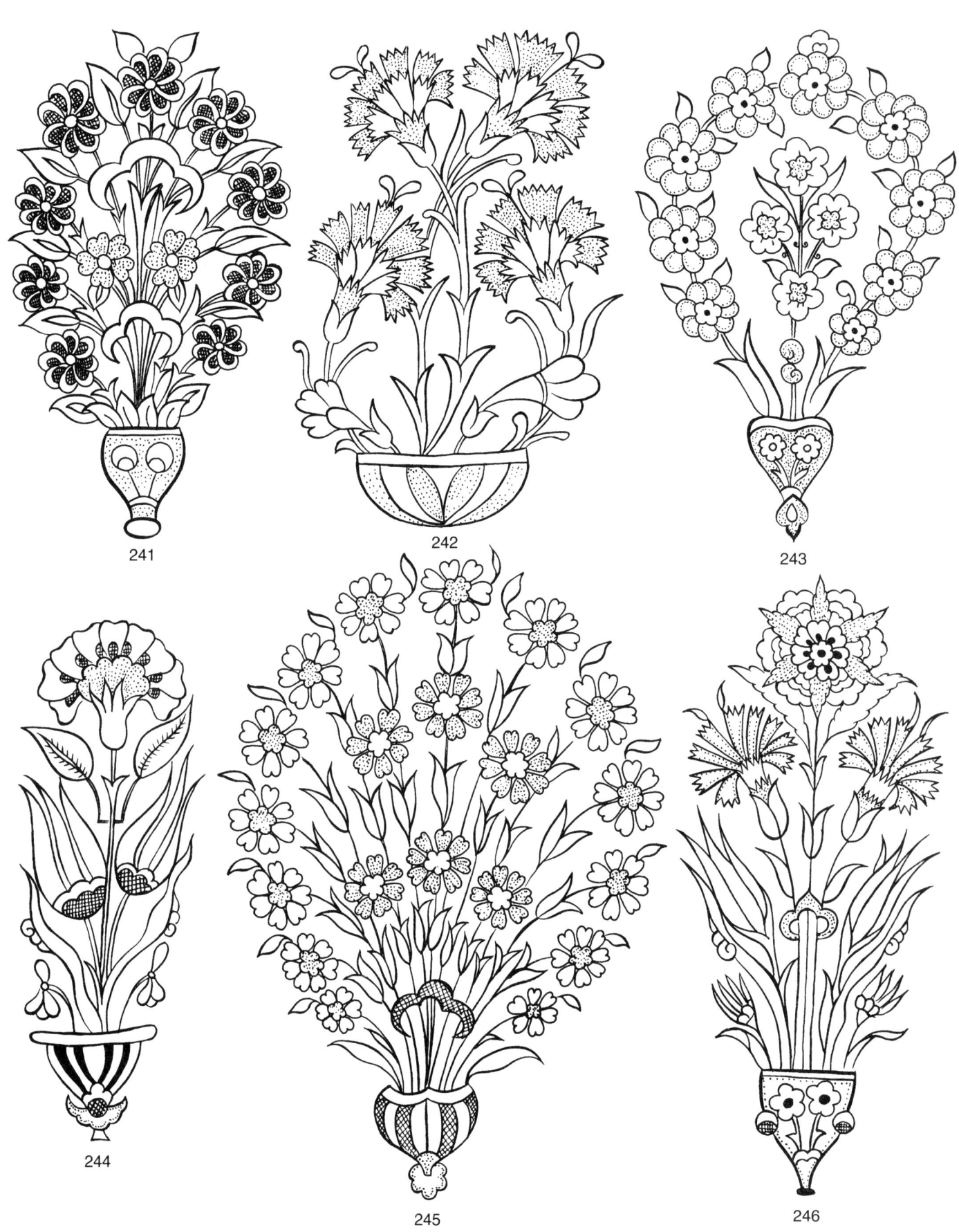

Vase and bouquet motifs

Designs with holy water flasks

Rumi scrolls (arabesques)

Rumi scrolls (arabesques)

Deer motifs

274

275

276

Rumi scrolls (arabesques)

Designs that radiate from a central point

Medallions

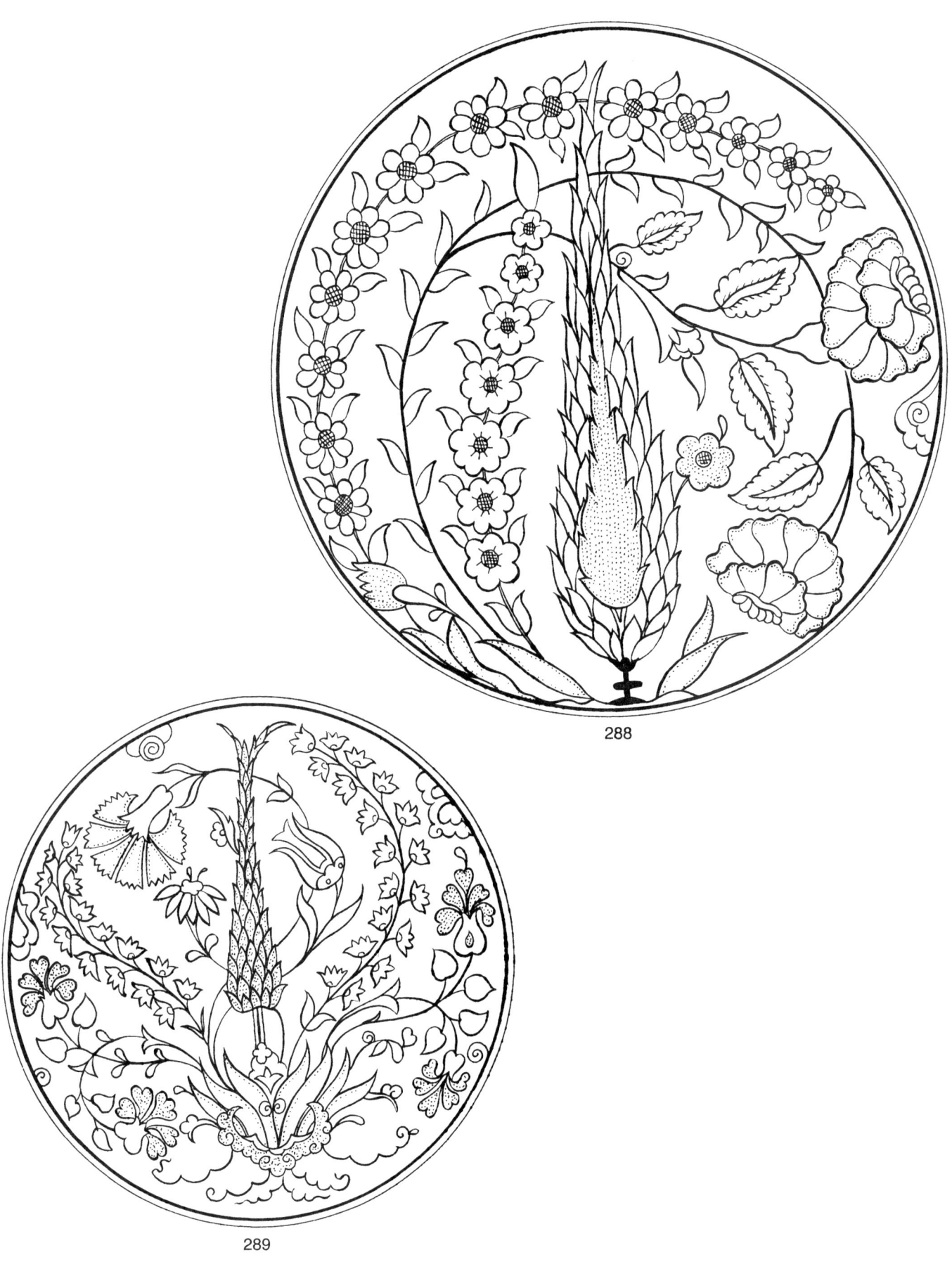

288

289

Cypress motifs

Sailing ship and galleon motifs

Sailing ship and galleon motifs

Fish motifs

Peacock motifs

Bird motifs

Dragon and phoenix designs

Dragon and phoenix designs

Harpy motifs

Human figures

Human figures